There are few poets who try to cover the arc of an entire life in a single volume; fewer still succeed. But *Summer Days at the Five and Dime* succeeds where few others do. Grunseth explores her life from toddler-on-a-trike through parent-of-adult-children with unflinching grace. Joys, sorrows, terrors and triumphs share these pages in tightly-woven lines that unfold a life story with simplicity and honesty. Pick it up when you have enough time for the whole book: you'll have trouble putting it down.

— **Peter Sherrill**, Co-poet-laureate of
Door County, Wisconsin 2025-27

Olly, Olly Oxen Free! If you run fast enough, the "it" won't get you, and the zest of life will fill you up until your entire life, all the moments, become poems that journey from childhood to old age and let everyone know just where you've been and how magic and tragic and scary and wonderful it's all been. Love, pain, fear, games, and history slicing like the prow of a canoe through deep waters. Annette Langlois Grunseth's new book of poetry, *Summer Days at the Five and Dime,* sings and jostles and laughs and cries as she comes up with poems that celebrate who she is, tells the story of the times she's lived, and then ends up summarizing time into the meaning of getting old. We all live a journey through a lifetime of moments and days, and in this book, echoes reverber-ate into the experiences we, the reader, have lived. And what a memorable journey that is!

— **Thomas and Ethel Mortenson Davis**, former Poet Laureates
of Door County, Wisconsin, authors of twenty-two books

Whether it is reflection or inspiration, Annette's poems take you to the everyday of a life. Remembering the long summer days of childhood, the struggle of becoming an adult, the waves of joy and sorrow that shape a life. Her words not only document a life well lived, but remind us to reexamine our own lives. Remind us that there is confusion, loss, contentment, love, and humor that make us who we have become. Remind us of the people we love and who love us. The things we tried. The success and the failure. The little differences that make us individuals.

In her words, we see her. In her sharing, we see ourselves.

— **Suzi Shapiro, PhD** and John Marshall School Alumna

Summer Days at the Five and Dime charms with its nostalgic look back at the touchstones of a life — childhood moments, turning points, and quiet revelations. What endures is the "person inside," "born of the stars" and "an arrow of curiosity," a self that keeps reaching toward wonder. These poems enchant with their fidelity to presence, to astonishment, to the everyday magic of being alive. They inhabit "a land where napkins fold themselves into swans," inviting readers to see the world anew. Created as a keepsake for family and friends, this collection is sure to become a cherished companion for anyone who opens its pages.

— **Tori Grant Welhouse,** author of
Padding Loamy on a Brew of Earth

What began as Annette Langlois Grunseth's legacy for her children and family, has evolved into a body of work encompassing a lifetime and pertinent to all readers. These poems celebrate a childhood filled with family, neighborhood and community. Happiness was the local Five and Dime; a quarter in your pocket, a penny on the sidewalk, or a box of 64 Crayola crayons. As she matures, the poems transform to show her deep connection to nature, her commitment to family and her concern for the environment. We, as readers, are invited to chuckle at her humor, feel her anxiety, identify with her losses, and share her hope for a bright future. Annette is a storyteller extraordinaire. *Summer Days at the Five and Dime* is evidence that our histories must not be forgotten. And that they need to be shared.

> — **Carrie Sherrill**, Co-Poet Laureate
> Door County, Wisconsin 2025-27

Virginia Woolf said the past is beautiful because one never realizes an emotion at the time, it expands later. And thus, nostalgia unlocks memories in *Summer Days at the Five and Dime* where Grunseth chronicles mid-century America. Strands of long-ago existence — saddle shoes, Cat's Eye marbles, red wax lips — reflect fun times with an inventive father and sensible mother, a brother, and later, the poet's husband and children.

This poet is made of light, evident in her awareness of twilight, street lights, dark room light, dust motes in sunlight, bright surgical lights, airport lights, and sugary light "wrapped in wonder, soft goodnight." Grunseth recalls that wonder, innocence, and mischief as she illuminates generational love, creating a homage for her lineage, but for you, too, who may yearn a lookback on your days and nights even as you live them.

> — **Kathryn Gahl**, Author of *Yes, No, I Don't Know*

Summer Days at the Five and Dime

POEMS BY

ANNETTE LANGLOIS GRUNSETH

ELM GROVE

"Happiness was the Five and Dime,
and a quarter in your pocket."
— Annette Langlois Grunseth

INTRODUCTION

I wrote these poems as a legacy for my children and family, to capture
what life was like growing up in the 1950s, 1960s, and beyond.

Before cell phones, before seat belts, before parents tracked our
every move, we were kids set loose in post–World War II central
Wisconsin. We belonged to the neighborhood. In summer, we left
after breakfast, came home for lunch and dinner, then ran back out
for night games until the streetlights flickered on and my mother's
three sharp blasts on her whistle called us home.

Nostalgia remembers long summer days, bike rides, and ice cream,
and sometimes forgets the harder truths.

We explored riverbanks, rode our bikes, tossed jacks, and played
Seven-Up, dress-up, and house. We built forts for "girls only," while
the boys played war, their staged battles fierce and vivid, as if the
whole world were their playground. Little did they know what lay
ahead. Just a few blocks away stood John Marshall School, lucky for
us that it was on our side of town.

Beyond our streets, the world was shifting: civil rights, Vietnam,
cultural upheaval. We felt it only at the edges, unaware of the weight
our parents carried.

These poems trace coming of age: learning freedom, discovering
friendship, and feeling the bonds of family, until the day we stepped
into lives of our own. From there, the book widens to include
adulthood and aging, when memory deepens, loss sharpens gratitude,
and time spent with water, woods, and music offers a way to listen
again. Together, the poems follow a life arc, shaped first by play and
possibility, and later by reflection, resilience, and attention to
what endures.

TABLE OF CONTENTS

A Touch of Winter

Growing Up and Liking It

The Day We Stepped into Lives of Our Own

Lessons and Legacies

Sandwiched Between

Rivers and Reflections

Epilogue

The Curious Years

I Am

born of the stars,
made with light and funny bones,
with naturally curly hair.
Mother said I was always
in motion, unruly as my hair.
I'm still tangled in a hectic life,
tethered to my mother roots,
yet aimed outward,
an arrow of curiosity,
a whirlwind of never enough.
I am fed by deep blue skies,
fire-red maples, and a full moon
that surfs the clouds at night.
I will always love fire-red maples
and deep blue skies
in a whirlwind of never enough.
Aimed outward, an arrow of curiosity,
I am tethered to mother-roots,
tangled in a hectic life,
always in motion, unruly as my hair,
made with light and funny bones.
I am born of the stars.

Annette, three years old

Olly, Olly Oxen Free

We played Robin Hood
in the forest across the street from our house
along the road past the old folks' home.
We trampled dirt paths down to the lake,
poked sticks in the water, hunted frogs,
explored like Davy Crockett
in our own wild frontier.
We spent hours along Lillie Street,
made up plays in the wooden gazebo
on Zirbel's Point.
We climbed the rafters to watch bats sleeping,
brushed spiders out of our hair,
screamed through the cobwebs.
On hot July afternoons
we braided long silk scarves together,
pinned them to the back of our short summer hair.
Like *National Velvet,* we rode our bikes,
which we swore were horses,
on paths through the field,
as wind blew through tall grass and our silky braids.
We rushed through dinner to run back outside for games,
Red Light, Green Light,
hope to see a ghost tonight;
Statue, and S.P.U.D.
When it grew dark, mother blew her whistle
three times to call us home.
Streetlights flickered on,
we chased each other in the twilight,
gasping to escape the ghost.
Olly, Olly Oxen Free!

Sleeve Sniffer

I never suck my thumb at night,
but sniff my sleeves instead.
I nuzzle close to cotton cuffs
and drift to sleep in bed.

My cuffs are cotton, smell of sun,
to sniff is the scent of sleep.
I bury my nose in the softest one,
it's better than counting sheep.

No *ba-ba,* no blankie,
to drag around with me.
When I slip into my jammies,`
my cuffs are all I need.

Hushed by habit, cozy bed,
sleeves are soft, smell just right.
I soothe away each fear or dread,
sniffed in comfort, tucked goodnight.

Annette, three years old

Summer Nights

Crickets chirp as dusk unfolds,
evening cool, the heat lets go.

A breeze appears, ever so slight
to calm me in the fading light.

I lie across the foot of my bed
window open, I rest my head.

On the sill, my stage to the sky,
a beacon turns at the airport nearby,

signals planes to touch down on land.
Green turns to white with each light band.

I watch the light with every sweep,
green … white … green … til I lift off to sleep.

Banana Split Moon

Pick a ripe banana moon from the sky,
peel it white, slice it lengthwise
over two scoops of clouds,

Sprinkle with stars,
and top with a caramel sun
dripping over the horizon.

Playing Paperboy

At four years old, I rule the morning street,
I ride my red trike, old news in a stack.
I pedal up the driveway, pump my feet.

From my basket, grab a paper, folded neat,
throw one on the porch, it lands with a smack.
At four years old, I rule the morning street.

Dad shoots a movie, tries to be discreet.
Play is my work, newspapers in the rack.
I pedal up the driveway, pump my feet.

I ride back down the sidewalk, then repeat,
toss more papers, turn around, come back.
At four years old, I rule the morning street.

Dad's paperboy game's a memory sweet.
The news is old, and time can't bring it back.
I pedal up the driveway, pump my feet.

Playing Dad's movie makes my days complete.
Looking back, I smile; there's nothing that I lack.
At four years old, I ruled the morning street,
I pedaled up the driveway, pumped my feet.

When I was Six

Blonde rays of summer hug my shoulders.
I sit in a cluster of buttercups,
I pick a handful, lick them, taste them.

I hope for butter
dripped over popcorn,
butter trickling a rounded mound
of mashed potatoes.
Yes! I taste butter,
melting into yeast-holes of bread.

In the grass, spread with yellow,
I lift a handful,
each small flower,
a buttered sun.

Ruptured – January 1955

It's a miracle I am here to tell this story. After seven decades, I can still see it, feel it, in the voice of a just-turned five-year-old.

Three days on the couch. My tummy hurts. I throw up in a bowl, again. Mother places a cool hand on my forehead and shakes down the glass thermometer. She talks to the doctor on the phone.

Suddenly, Dad scoops me up in my pink pajamas, wraps me in a blanket, and carries me to the old gray Plymouth. We drive quickly to the hospital at the end of Sturgeon Eddy Road, a short distance from our house.

Bright lights glare, big as dinner plates. A black rubber mask covers my nose and mouth. Something bitter and cold drips in. Ether. I try to pull the mask away, but many hands hold me down.

When I wake, clowns dance on the walls. Red suits with polka dots. Yellow curls. Ruffled collars. A three-ring circus spins across the room. I don't understand why I must lie still.

[Later, I learn what happened to me. My appendix had burst. The doctor cut into my right side, removed the remains, poured raw penicillin into the open incision to stop infection, left a drain, and stitched me up. They feared peritonitis.]

They place me in a white crib that feels like a cage. The metal bars clink when I move. Cribs are for babies, but I am five. A big girl.

They roll me into a ward filled with boys and park me by a big window across from the nurses' station so they *can see me better.*

Every day brings needles and thermometers. The glass thermometer soaks in alcohol. Morning and night, shots go into one butt cheek, then the other. Penicillin. After two weeks, my bottom burns. Then they switch me to pills that get caught in my throat.

Together in the ward, the boys yell. One boy's leg hangs in a cast from the ceiling. Another's arm is plastered straight up in the air. When they holler, the nurses snap at them to be quiet. I lie still and watch.

One day, two nurses wheel in a cart with brown tubes and needles. They wrap my arms and legs in rubber tubing and push needles through the tubes, then into me, again and again. I scream. They say it doesn't hurt. But it does.

The boys yell louder. A nurse snaps, *Be quiet or you'll be next.*

I fall silent.

People bring presents. *Madeline,* a book about a girl who had her appendix out just like me. A lady-head vase with straw flowers. A small wooden birdhouse with a bird that sings when you turn a knob.

Daddy comes after work every day. He reaches through the crib bars, and we play *Chick-in-the-Coop.* I snap the spinner, move the chick five spaces. I count carefully. Snap again, move three spaces.

I talk to Daddy. I talk to Mommy. I do not talk to the nurses.

No one tells me how to ask for the bathroom while trapped in a crib. The boys shout. Nurses wheel them away. I'm too scared to call out. When the sheets are wet, I'm scolded.

It feels like forever. Then one day, Mother says I can go home.

At home, Mother gives me a sponge bath. She peels off the gauze bandage taped to my side. I stare at black stitches pulling the pucker of my skin. The scar is a red line.

In the fall, I start kindergarten. I don't talk to anyone. I follow the rules. The teachers think something is wrong.

A psychologist tells Mother to wait. *One day,* he says, *she will tell you.*

In spring, the story spills out: the crib, the needles, the tubes, the yelling boys, the stitches, the clowns.

By first grade, I learn to read. I make friends. I talk. Too much.

I've been making up for lost time ever since.

Epilogue

The next year, I had my tonsils out. They gave me penicillin, and my body erupted in hives; red, itchy, angry. The doctor warned that next time it could be anaphylaxis. I was told never to take penicillin again.

Antibiotics. Surgery. Science. They saved my life. Without them, my children would never have been born.

Sunday Funnies

We are nestled in the brown, loopy couch,
his arm curved around me,
snug in my pink pajamas.
Dad reads the Sunday funnies aloud.

We tumble into *Blondie's* full-color world,
Dagwood napping on his couch
or building his signature sandwich.
Some days, Dad and I
stack our own towers of bread,
too high to fit our wide-open mouths.

I loved *Priscilla's Pop* and her friend Hollyhock,
and their mashed potato sandwiches.
It's the way Dad said, Hollyhock.
I can hear him now, *Hollyhock said …*

And Mother from the other room
warning, *Mashed potato sandwiches*
aren't healthy — too much starch.

Dancing with Dad

The needle lightly touches
the edge of the spinning 78
and with a soft crackle,
music fills the room.

Dad pulls me in close,
I step onto his shoes,
my small feet perched
on his size fourteens.

He waltzes me in smooth circles,
one, two, three … one, two, three …
my arm stretches left in his,
the other hand warm at his waist.

We glide across the living room,
sway to the rhythm —
two feet on top of two feet,
spinning through childhood.

Pencil Hoarder

Hidden under mail in the kitchen,
beneath old magazines on the coffee table,
and tangled in chaos on the tea cart
that never served tea,
I searched for pencils.

I looked for long ones, stubby ones,
sharpened or broken-tipped,
red, blue, and yellow number twos.
I collected pencils from banks,
hardware stores, lumberyards
with black or gold advertising on their barrels.
Some had tooth marks
from too much figuring.

A hoarder in a house of clutter,
I lined them up in rows on my windowsill.
The beveled ones kept the round ones still.
Leaded ends pointed north, erasers south.
My parents (and my brother)
crept in at night to "borrow" from my stash,
since I was rich in pencils,
and always ready to draw pictures,
or print my name from the wealth
on my windowsill.

A Scar for Life

The day I fell off my bike,
and the sidewalk slammed my face,
I lay there, like a stunned bird,
until my brother carried me home,
my just-grown-in-front teeth
dangling by their roots.

In the elevator to the dentist's office,
strangers stared at the crimson handkerchief
I held to my face.

The exam room smelled of tooth polish and antiseptic.
The dentist bent close, gentle hands
pushed my teeth back into their sockets,
anchored them in place with a thin silver wire.

For six weeks I ate baby food,
mashed bananas, creamy oatmeal,
and milkshakes, sipped cold and smooth
through a straw.

When the scab on my lip
peeled and dropped away,
I fingered the tender nick.

Now that pale crease in my skin,
always there in the mirror,
disappears whenever I smile.

Santa Arrives by Airplane

At the airport, we kids feel magic in the air.
A plane circles overhead, our faces squint skyward,
fingers looping through the fence links.

A Piper Cub banks around,
touches down, taxies to a gate.
With a hearty *Ho-Ho-Ho,*

Santa, white beard, red suit, black boots,
climbs from the plane with a brown sack
bulging over his shoulder.

His sleigh waits on the runway.
Two reindeer paw the ground,
puffs of white fog curling from their nostrils.

On Dancer, on Dasher! Santa shouts.
The reindeer pull forward, the sleigh glides,
the parade begins.

So much magic in the air,
we never doubted.

Wish on a Penny

The summer I was eight, I wished on a penny for a black kitten. That autumn, while partridge hunting, Dad found a clump of black fur beneath a nest of leaves, yellow marble eyes peering out and a mew so weak he nearly missed it. Light as a songbird, Dad pocketed a kitten in his vest as the dog raced past, partridge in mouth.

At home, he drew the kitten from his pocket, all bones and breath, set her on the kitchen floor. She lapped milk from a saucer. I named her Inky, a child's simple thought-up name. She slept on my bed in the sun but hissed when dressed in baby clothes and tucked into a doll crib. She preferred the sun, the heat grate, or my older brother's quiet lap, where they dozed together, too tired even for bed.

She peed in the galoshes that went over Dad's shoes, a sour surprise when he left for work. We drank skim milk; Inky got "whole." On muffled feet, she galloped to the kitchen at the whir of the can opener, for nineteen years.

she prowls the night
black as sleep
morning mouse on the step

Blue Willow Days

A child's table is set for three,
little teacups, saucers, plates, and a tiny teapot.

Blue Willow china, miniatures
of cobalt trees bow over arched bridges.

Pagodas rise from white china,
birds glide through painted light.

Coalie, one-eyed and well-loved sits beside
Virginia the doll, dressed for tea at half past pretend.

We sip water from tea cups that never spill,
and nibble grahams spread with butter, never too full.

We practice please and thank you, pinkies raised,
chase stories down the rabbit hole of fantasy.

The jam grows jealous of butter on the grahams,
in a land where napkins fold themselves into swans.

We take our tea plain or with a lump of sugar,
stir made-up tales into the air.

Then Coalie and Virginia nod off like dormice,
curled over crumbs left on their plates.

The lid closes on the teapot of pretend,
cups and saucers are washed and dried.

Each piece settled into its secure box,
the clink of make-believe still warm.

Oh, those Blue Willow days!

Coalie and Virginia take tea on a Blue Willow day.

Around the
world with my
View-Master

Transported

I slide *Tomorrowland* into the slot,
the future in my hands.
I look through the eyepieces,
pull-click… pull-click… around the wheel.
I'm at *Disneyland,* its tiny monorail
circles visitors toward the Matterhorn.
I hold a mountain of memories
in these 3-D pictures.

Pull-click…pull-click…
seven scenes round the wheel.
I'm with dinosaurs in Utah one day,
hiking the Grand Canyon the next.

I cock each square of the reel forward,
explore sampans in Hong Kong,
a pagoda in Tiger Balm Gardens.
Pull-click… pull-click…
around the wheel, around the world.

When I grow tired of Hong Kong,
I go to *Wild Animals of West Africa,*
then visit all *Seven Wonders of the World,*
from the Pyramids of Egypt, to Mt. Rushmore,
to the Taj Mahal, all the while sitting
on my bedroom floor, ankle over ankle,
transported through my View-Master.

Shoes, Secrets, and Summer Days

Darkroom

Dad leads me into the red glow
of the safe light behind the black curtain.
He shows me how —
projects beams of white light
through a negative onto glossy photo paper.

He counts:
one, one-thousand;
two, one-thousand;
three one-thousand; four —
then snaps off the light.

He lets me slide the exposed paper
into a white enamel pan of developer.
Together we rock it gently
as waves roll through chemicals,
until the ghost of an image rises,
our family at the piano.

Dad stands to the left
in a suit and tie,
my brother in pressed pants
and a white shirt.
I sit beside Mother on the piano bench,
petti-coated dress, white anklets,
and black *Mary Janes.*

A book of carols lies open on my lap.
Mother, in a white blouse
with black velveteen flowers,
sits next to me in a dark skirt,
her legs crossed at the ankles.
This image becomes us
forever.

Christmas 1958

Dad's Vise

After a long day at the office, Dad settled in the basement rec room, seated at an old door laid across two file cabinets. A C-clamp anchored a small vise to the makeshift bench. The metal barrel narrowed to a silver cone. Its teeth, a miniature jaw, held the smallest fishhook for tying handmade flies.

Shoeboxes, light as air, held brown feathers. Others smelled of mothballs, stuffed with deer tails dyed red, yellow, and black, stacked beside him. Wooden spools of thread, a spectrum of color flowed like a river across the bench.

He snipped fur from a bucktail, selected a feather, tightened a hook in grooves of the vise. Pinching a tuft of fur, he added a feather to the shaft, winding metallic thread around and around in stripes to mimic a Mayfly hatch or minnow.

Half-knots cinched thread to the Jigger-Diggers. He trimmed deer tail fur to shape the Mayflies. For the Nymphs and Spinners, a coat of nail polish sealed thread over fur. He took art classes to learn sketching, designed his own mail order catalogs, sold his lures around the world.

My dad, Al Langlois, ties fishing flies by hand

his "vise" a virtue
each hand-tied lure
a catch of art

Foundations

My big-bosomed great aunts
brought the latest fashions
to their general store
in small-town Minnesota.
They were women of *foundations*,
who wore armored brassieres
with rows of sturdy hooks,
corsets laced tight as oxfords.

Their tailored dresses bore big lapels,
shoulder pads, and brooches pinned over their hearts,
wide-brimmed hats tilted just so,
white gloves poised for proper hands.

They had opinions about conduct, gifted me
Etiquette for Young People by Emily Post
and the *Fanny Farmer Junior Cookbook*.
They tutored me in manners and meal-making.

When I visited, I'd better have a lace hankie
and white gloves in my purse.
Instead, my fingers squished
garden dirt into water,
slapped mud pies down the driveway,
just to see their faces.

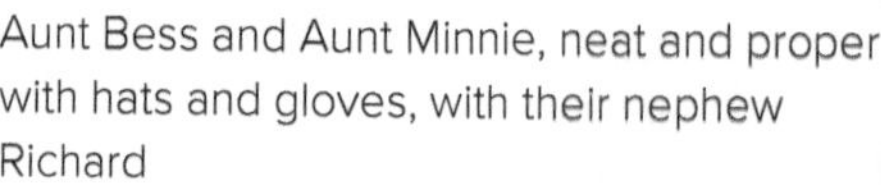

Aunt Bess and Aunt Minnie, neat and proper
with hats and gloves, with their nephew
Richard

White Socks

My grandfather, the dentist,
sneaks me sugar cubes
from the china bowl on the table,
behind the back of his disapproving wife.

Sweetness dissolves on my tongue.
Grandy stashes a handful
in the cavity of his pocket.
We head out for the afternoon

to the barn where he boards his horse.
The wood door judders,
we tug it open just enough
to slip into the dim light.

Flecks of dust and hay float
in slatted sunlight.
Bridles dangle from pegs,
saddles clasp a railing.

The air smells of straw
and sweat-stained leather.
White Socks snorts our arrival
from the last stall at the far left.

Hold your hand flat and open — like this.
Grandy sets three cubes in my palm.
Nostrils flare. Huge horsey lips
nudge and nibble my fingers.

I flinch.
Grandy steadies me,
wet velvet nuzzles sugar
from my open hand.

White Socks, a retired
circus horse, poses with my
grandfather, Ingvald Bergh, DDS

South Dakota – 1961

Grandy cinches the saddle's wide strap.
White Socks inhales; the girth expands – unnoticed.
Snort! The clever horse exhales,
the saddle slips to the side.
Grandy cinches again, chuckles, pats the mane.
With Grandy's boost, my leg swings up and over.

I settle into the saddle, my stomach flutters.
He adjusts the stirrups to my long legs,
shows me how to weave the reins
through my fingers, one hand only.
I drape them lightly across White Socks' neck
to guide him left or right.

Don't pull too hard, he warns–
the bit can hurt the horse's mouth.
We circle the corral twice.
Then Grandy lets go.
White Socks walks, then quickens to a trot.
I bounce like popcorn in a hot pan, teeth rattling.

I stiffen, white-knuckle the reins.
Relax, you're doing fine, Grandy calls.
I squeeze with my thighs,
click my tongue to giddyup.

Lean into the gait, he shouts.
And suddenly –
we lift together into a smooth canter,
the rhythm of heat and muscle,
thud of hooves on the grass,
wind riffles my hair.

Grandy calls from behind:
You're a natural on a horse.

White Socks with my
grandfather, Grandy.

Summer Days at the Five and Dime

At the end of Kent Street
on the other side of Grand Avenue
Ohland's Ben Franklin, Five and Dime, beckons.

You ride your blue bike,
a quarter shoved in your pocket,
with an itch to spend it.

Should you buy *Lik-M-Aid,*
Pixy Stix, Jawbreakers,
or *Bazooka* – for the comics?

Instead, you splurge on red wax lips
and a black wax mustache,
ten cents each.

The leftover nickel buys
a miniature six-pack
of wax bottles filled with nectar.

You bite off the caps,
suck out the sweet juice,
then chew the wax into a squishy ball.

Bite the soft blob,
peel the wax from your teeth,
inspect your tooth prints.

Happiness is
the *Five and Dime,*
a quarter in your pocket.

Don't Lose It

I slip the hollow end
over the metal nub that juts out,
turn the key; tighten toe clamps
over the edges of my saddle shoes.

I buckle leather straps snug 'round my ankles,
push off from the porch steps,
shift one leg to the other,
picking up speed in smooth arcs.

Arms swing wide, knees bend,
legs pump, each stride
a blur of speed, wheels scrape
and spark on concrete.

I orbit the blocks like Sputnik,
skate down Kent, past Kusel's house,
left on Zimmerman, wave to Wally the mailman.
Cut over on Ross to the Dairy Queen on Grand
a dime in my pocket for a swirl of vanilla.

Summer of skinned knees,
I chase endless sidewalks,
the skate key swings on a loop of twine.
Around my neck, I feel its tug at every turn —
Still there.
Still there.

Skate keys on a string, don't lose them!

Circle in the Dirt

My brother carries a cloth sack, cinched with an old shoelace, hooked to his blue-jeaned belt loop. Inside: Purees, cobalt blue, green, and gold; Cat's Eyes, pupils slit in yellow or blue. The shooter, heavy with anticipation, is twice the size of the rest.

On the playground, a circle is drawn in the dirt. Marbles tumble into the circle as boys empty their bags. One knee down, hand to the ground, my brother cocks a glass shooter at his thumbnail, pressed against the forefinger. Snap! The shooter arcs toward a Cat's Eye or a prized Aggie. A crack splits the air, and a marble shoots across the circle. Each boy has a turn aiming their Steelie or glass shooter until the circle is cleared. What is knocked from the circle is earned. Some leave with hollow pouches light with loss, others carry treasures that clink with pride.

Marble tournaments continue until the best players face off at the end of May, the winner announced after lunch on the school PA to thunderous cheers.

setting sun shoots light
above clouds
marbled pink and blue

Fooling the Tooth Fairy

Goosebumps rise as I peer into the empty eye sockets.

My grandfather was a dentist, retired now. So is the human skull
that sits on my brother's dresser next to a jackknife and a Boy Scout
handbook.

My finger traces brittle bone,
forehead to empty nose hole, along the jaw —
The skull moves!

I pull back — heart pulsing in my ears.

A tooth rattles loose, another, and another.
I gather loose teeth like beach pebbles, never satisfied with just one,
cup them in my hand until I have sixteen teeth.

Aha! A dime for each one from the Tooth Fairy.
Imagine, sixteen shiny dimes — a dollar sixty!

I count them again and tuck the teeth under my pillow.
At dinner I boast, *I'm going to fool the Tooth Fairy and get rich.*

Pop laughs, tears at the corners of his eyes. Why is he laughing?
Doesn't he know this is serious Tooth Fairy business?

Wait until I show you a fistful of dimes tomorrow morning.

With I-can't-wait-excitement, I curl into the covers.
One last check under the pillow, then I drift off.

Morning nudges me awake, I jerk upright, lift the pillow —

Sixteen teeth. Just as I left them.
No dimes, just teeth.

All these years later, I know what happened.
Pop snitched on me.

Nunn-Bush Shoe Store

We trip the bell at Nunn-Bush Shoes on Third Street. The smell of leather and polish greets us. Dread tightens in my chest as Mother asks for brown oxfords with steel arch supports. We sit in a row of anchored theater seats across from the clerk's low, slanted stool. Mother says she doesn't want me to have bad feet, that support matters, but all I want are red Keds.

I stand on the metal foot measurer, cold numbers and lines beneath me. The clerk notes my growth, slips behind a curtain, returns with a box, peels back the tissue, and lifts a brown lace-up shoe; its leather sole is stiff and hard.

Straddling the slanted stool, he threads the laces through neat rows of eyelets, slides the shoe on with a cold metal horn, and tugs the laces snug.

Mother presses her thumb to the toe. Room to grow? I step onto the fluoroscope. Purple x-rays glow. My ghost bones wiggle and shift inside the shoes, just shy of the ends. A perfect fit, she says.

At the counter, my feet trapped in stiff brown oxfords, I ask Mother for a penny for the gumball machine.

coin in the slot
lever turns, please
let it be the blue one

I Stand Corrected

Boxy toes, sturdy soles, brown-ugly oxfords.
Mother said, *You'll thank me one day.*
Kids in arch-less Keds and ballet flats tease me,
Boy shoes! Boy shoes!

I stuff my green suede gym shoes in a grocery sack,
carry them to school under my arm. The boy shoes
get ditched beneath the backyard bushes.
I change into my worn-out gym shoes.

After school, I crawl back under the shrubs,
swap into the brown-uglies
scuttle to the basement
to start my *homework.*

Scuff and scrape, scrape and scuff —
brown-uglies against the concrete floor,
wear 'em down to holes in the soles.
Snip, snip the top stitching with Mom's manicure scissors.

Wear them out. Wear them out.
Until ... she says, *Your shoes are in shambles.*
We're off to Wally's Shoe Repair on 6th.
He re-soles, re-stitches, and buffs them smooth

with a fresh coat of Oxblood Red,
a name that turns my stomach.
My hard work undone. I begin again.
Scuff, scrape, snip, snip.

Breaking Mother's rules just to fit in.
Today, cute lady shoes torment my fallen arches.
Men's hiking boots with beefy orthotics, give relief,
still tripping over Mother's words.

Bully

From behind me I hear *HRRRK!*
A yellow gob of spit hits
my tan suede jacket
with shiny buttons the size of nickels.
I watch the hawked gob
ooze down my new jacket,
the one my mother bought me
for the start of third grade.

I almost retch onto the sidewalk.
He does it again, *HRRRK.*
This one hits my sleeve,
slime-yellow trickles toward my wrist.
I stifle a heave.
He's in fifth grade,
has a bunch of brothers, all big kids.
He grins through yellow teeth.

He follows me. I turn away,
walk along Ross Avenue,
head over on Zimmerman toward home.
The thick spit soaks into the suede,
dark brown spots spread into large, wet circles.
I turn the corner to my street.
He takes off down another street
laughing.

Crayola Cravings

It began with a Jumbo box of eight chubby crayons — primary colors plus green, brown, black, orange, and purple. Our Kindergarten fists learned how to grip and color, mostly outside the lines. First Grade, we graduated to the box of twelve, neatly lined in two rows.

As we grew, we wanted more. If we were lucky, our parents surprised us with the box of twenty-four with names that felt exotic: carnation pink, dandelion, cerulean.

Next came the compact tower of forty-eight with the flip top lid. Crayons stood like choristers on risers, tilted for easy choosing: blue-green (my favorite), teal blue (was there a difference?), maize, raw umber, violet-red, and burnt sienna. I touched the perfect points. Each papered stick smelled of wax, back-to-school, autumn, heaven.

We colored maps; melted crayon shavings between waxed paper for "stained glass" taped to classroom windows. As the year wore on, we peeled wrappers to reveal more wax, slid the shortened stubs back into their slots.

By fifth grade, we begged for the Cadillac of crayons: the box of sixty-four. Magenta, periwinkle, melon, mulberry, midnight blue — and always, burnt sienna.

But the real treasure? The sharpener built into the back of the box.

The Cousins Come for a Visit

We slept on air mattresses in the den, the accordion door closed between us and the living room where our mothers whispered. Their voices rose and fell, a duet of memory and suspicion, piecing together a family secret. My grandmother's father died from diabetes; no treatment was available then. There was a stepfather when she was a teen.

leaves of three
let it be
poison ivy spreads

When I knew her, Grandma kept her curtains drawn. She was cold and prickly and needed mud-thick coffee to wake up in the morning. She said Grandy's snoring drove her to her own room, her own bed. Maybe it was more than that, they wondered.

By morning, our mothers' voices were raw, the mystery unsolved. *You're wearing yesterday's clothes,* my cousin said. That's when we knew they'd stayed up all night trying to open the door to a secret.

sensitive plant
feathery leaves shut tight
when touched

The World at Our Fingertips

When we wanted to know, our "search engine" was the *World Book Encyclopedia.* Sold door to door, they were an investment in your child's education and *their very future.* Twenty hardcover volumes arrived, deep red faux leather with navy and gold embossed letters on each spine. They filled an entire shelf in the den. Shiny pages smelled of ink and gloss, and the spines cracked when opened. History. Science. Geography. Medicine. The body, with diagrams! My cousins had the newer edition, cream-colored covers with forest green and gold lettering. We poured over those books from cover to cover.

Each year brought a new volume. When the Yearbook arrived, we gathered with clean hands, always clean hands. Fingers turning pages, we inhaled the sharp scent of ink. Wide-eyed, we read about new diseases, outer space, and inventions that seemed to glow with science fiction. Then we slid it carefully onto the shelf, right where it belonged – after W–Z.

the human body
clear plastic overlays
bone, muscle, maze of veins

Carrot Capers

Our neighbor works in her garden
in the cooling-off evenings of July.
Wooden planks outline
feathered rows of carrots.
Mrs. Traeger squats
on those boards after supper
pulling weeds row after row,
her trowel poking at the soil
of her manicured garden.

When she goes inside,
we neighborhood kids roam
the backyards at twilight,
sneak into her garden,
snatch a few carrots.
We knock off chunks of dirt
slapping the carrots against each other.
We scrub the orange tapers on our shorts,
bite off an end with a crisp snap,
the taste of sweet mischief on our tongues.

Rugosa Rose

grew tall and full
cornered outside my brother's bedroom window.
That rose bush grew as unruly as us kids
who ran free on summer days.

Coiled behind this gangly shrub,
we tugged the green garden hose out to the yard.
One of us squeezed behind those dense prickers,
cranked the faucet wide open.

Thorns caught a shirt,
snagged skin,
a gash of blood trickled down an arm,
soon red-crusted by the sun.

Water on full blast,
the hose gushed into our mouths
with a faint taste of rubber
and the aroma of rose.

Dress-Up

We ask our mothers for their cast-off clothes — dresses, skirts, old
purses, and their worn-out high heels. Becky pulls on her mother's
red and white plaid dress; its torn hem brushes the ground. At age
eleven, my large feet squeeze into my mother's nine and a half heels.
Her beige purse hangs askew in my right hand, Becky's mother's
handbag dangles in her left. Long stick pins fasten veiled hats to our
heads, and I drape a weird tulle shawl.

at the river
blue herons
preen their feathers

We clomp in heels down the sidewalk, play *Ladies' Aid*, gather on the
front steps of a neighbor who we hope is not home. We sit outside
their door on the top step, whisper about the next potluck and a bake
sale. We adjourn, close our purses, adjust our skirts, and clack our
heels home.

evening breeze
rose-tinted hydrangeas
brush the bedroom screen

Annette and Becky, 11, play
dress-up

Cloudy, with a Chance of Disaster

Storms brewed inside my mother,
spun a funnel of fear
imported from the South Dakota prairie.
She remembered the *dirty thirties:*

school dismissed at noon,
sky black as midnight,
street lights on at midday,
wet handkerchiefs pressed to their faces
as they slanted home into the dirt-filled wind.

Her mother stuffed wet towels
along the window sills,
but the dirt blew in anyway;
covered counters, plates, and pillows.
The prairie picked itself up,
and ground fear into her bones.

Years later in Wisconsin,
Mother watched the sky,
studied the barometer on the dining table.
When the pressure dropped to twenty-nine
she'd scan the heavens for *mares tails,*
a sure sign doom was headed our way.

One night as sirens blared,
Mother herded us to the basement,
ordered my Dad to hook up
a garden hose to the washtub faucet
ready for the firestorm sure to follow the twister.

We huddled under the stairs,
half afraid, half rolling our eyes.
As the freight train of a tornado skimmed west of town,
it lifted, as if by a miracle,
up and over Rib Mountain.

Next morning dawned peaceful and sunny,
my brother shouted, *It's a beautiful day!*
Barometer in hand, Mother warned,
But it's going to get worse.

Fear, Head On

Walking home from school
a dog stands in the middle of the sidewalk,
big, yellow, fierce.
He bares his teeth, snarling.

I smell my own fear.
We look at each other.
We have two hunting dogs at home,
so I know dogs can sniff fear.

I stand my ground,
look at the dog's eyes, then look away.
I know better than to stare down a dog.
I am not afraid. I am not afraid.

The dog growls again,
shows his big teeth,
the kind that can bite,
even tear flesh.

I look away, walk slowly past the mutt.
one foot in front of the other.
I do not run.
I am not afraid. I am not afraid.

Big, yellow, fierce,
he stands in the middle of the sidewalk
as I walk home from school.

Where Maples Grew

Two dozen, fifty-year-old
heavy-bosomed maple trees
shaded my childhood home,
casting coolness across our yard.
The leafy giants lined Kent Street
with their arch of shelter and shade.

Each maple grew taller, thicker with age,
big enough to hide behind
for *Red Light, Green Light* on a summer night.
In autumn they draped yellow light over us
before dropping heaps of leaves for jumping.

Under a plot of progress with traffic rising,
a widened street was planned,
the trees were slated to go.
My enraged mother gathered signatures,
spoke out at city hall, wrote letters to the editor:
Save our half-centenarians!
Sadly, the city architects of progress won.

Father, with his movie camera,
filmed that day when bulldozers arrived
to yank out each maple like a giant tooth,
huge roots exposed, lying on their sides,
our mouths gaping at the extraction.

The Father of Modification
(kin to the Mother of Invention)

If Dad owned it, he modified it.
He weighted his Kroydon golf club irons with lead,
lengthened their handles to match his reach,
then re-wrapped the grips in layers of improvement.

He tore the seats out of his van,
built an extra-long, wood bed frame,
added a folding lawn chair,
his idea of comfort on wheels.

He designed and tied his own fishing lures,
then sketched them in art classes at the university
to create a mail-order catalog sent across the world
under the name Lang Lure Co.

He sawed his old hickory downhill skis
into cross-country slivers, sanded,
stained, and waxed them with paraffin.
(I still have mine.)

At Mother's black Singer, he fed Dacron through the machine,
sewing sails for a seventeen-foot canoe, while winter
iced-over the windows. He varnished lee boards smooth,
bolted them to the gunnels so his tippy canoe held steady in wind.

The stone fireplace he once built five feet high
for grilling was later cut to half its height for campfires, too.
He screwed a mini-tripod into trees
for self-timed photographs, the first "selfies."

He stacked two pairs of magnifying readers
to invent his own trifocals. When his hearing went,
he rejected a hearing aid, wore headphones
hooked to a cheaper, neck-dangling amplifier instead.

He never met an object he couldn't improve.
Everything he touched became one-of-a-kind.

My dad, Al Langlois, designed and sewed the sails on my mother's Singer, creating a one-of-a-kind sailing canoe.

The Paint Was Still Wet

A summer Saturday in 1961, Dad painted the full slat garage door of our single-stall garage and left it raised to let the paint dry. Inside the garage sat our old gray Plymouth that Mother named Tin Lizzie. Our cat slept in the rafters, using the open door as a springboard to come and go.

She woke from her nap, sprang onto the freshly painted door, padded across it, then bounded onto the roof of Tin Lizzie. From there she walked across the roof, tiptoed down the driver's side window, and pranced over the hood leaving pawprints of white paint. The ones across the windshield were scraped off, but the rest stayed; a custom paint job.

rabbit tracks
path to evergreens
raisins in the snow.

Tall Kid Problems

Neighbor Dad:
Go play with someone your own age.
(I *am!* Your kid's my age)

Group photos:
You, there, go to the back row.
(Just a floating head in the crowd)

Choir risers:
Top row for you.
(One wrong move, it's a long way down)

Desks:
Take the last row, last seat, in the back.
(Squints at the chalkboard in a fog)

Dance class, junior high:
Line up by height.
(At last — first in something)

A Touch of Winter

December 1959

The first snowfall of the year. Giant snowflakes were falling all afternoon outside the tall windows of our third-grade classroom. At our desks, working, I kept popping up to peek out the window to see how deep it was getting. I had butterflies in my stomach, thinking about skiing at Rib Mountain all day on Saturday.

Sit down, Annette, the teacher scolded me more than once.
But the snow kept whispering to me,
ski, ski, ski.

Best Night of the Year

Dad brings me back to school after dinner.
Windows at John Marshall School glow
warm against the snow.
We climb the steps
into classrooms turned carnival,
the PTA in full bloom.

A few dimes and a quarter
buy a string of red tickets.
In the third grade classroom, Mrs. Yensh
stands before a hanging bedsheet.
I cast my line over the top —
a tug, a bite,
I reel in a Duncan yo-yo!

Goldfish circle in bowls of water
dyed pink, yellow and blue
in the fourth grade room.
I get three ping pong balls
for one ticket.
One bounces off the rim
and chatters across the floor.
One teeters, falls.
One lands lucky,
kersplash in the center.

Cake-walk squares
taped to the school kitchen floor.
Music plays. We march,
heels tapping past decorated cakes,
until the tune stops,
hoping to land on the lucky number.

Paper plates bend under cake and frosting.
Snow reflects the bright lights.
Goldfish swim home in plastic bags.

We Could Skate All Day

The fire department floods
the school playground
into a sheet of thin ice.
A green wooden warming house
leans at the edge.
Inside, it huffs oil heat and wet wool.

I walk with neighborhood kids,
to school on Saturday.
Skates slung around our necks,
laces knotted, blades bump against our chests.
Boots thud to the floor.
We pull laces tight until our ankles ache.
Stow boots under the wood benches.

At the candy counter, Mr. B slides boxes
of Raisinets, red ropes of licorice, and Milk Duds
in exchange for our nickels and dimes.
Outside, a speaker blares tinny music
that crackles across the rink.

We skate clockwise at first
in slow circles.
Blades scrape snow dust across the ice.
Summeone skates backwards,
another shoots to the center
to spin in the wide-open space.

We clomp back in to warm up,
mittens steam against the heater,
our fingers tingle back to life.
All afternoon, we circle
the hard skin of ice,
practice figure eights.

When day turns to dusk
we change into our boots
to walk home.
Cheeks burn,
legs wobble,
and ankles throb,
still tracing lines in the ice.

Growing Up and Liking It

What We Weren't Told

We're ushered to the A-V room in fourth grade
clutching empty pocket folders.
The teacher gave each one of us a booklet:
Growing Up and Liking It.

In the dimmed room we watch a filmstrip,
follicles push an egg
slowly along a fallopian tube.
A girl is in tears every month.
And there's blood?

Why is she crying?
What's the big secret?
What's happening?

The lights flicker on.

Before we file back to our classroom
the teacher makes us
hide the pamphlets
in our pocket folders.

Back in class, we wonder …
What were the boys told
when they went to the gym
and returned empty-handed?

The Secret

After school, under the old maple tree
on the front lawn, my best friend
places the palm of her hand
against the bark of the trunk.

She presses her lips
to the back of her hand,
and makes mushy kiss noises
like in the movies,
to show what we can do with boys.

Then, she tells me a big secret —
we both scream,
cross our hearts,
promise we'll never get married.
Never. Ever.

Birds, Bees, and Flowers

My best friend told me.
I'm shocked.
I ask my mother,
Can this be true?

She dries her hands
on the apron tied to her waist,
goes to the bookshelves in the den,
heavy with the classics, Shakespeare,
and a long row of red-spined
World Book Encyclopedia.

She pulls out a thin book from the top shelf
that her mother gave to her,
hands it to me with no explanation,
and heads back to the kitchen.

I lie on my bed, read about
flowers, stamens, pistils,
pollen falling into crevices —
What do flowers have to do with me?

It's a miracle I'm here at all.

Junior High Gym Class

We wear the required light green, short-legged, one-piece cotton gym suit with elastic at the waist, cap sleeves, and snaps down the front. We jog a circle in the gym. Sit-ups, elbows to knees. We're supposed to climb a thick rope dangling from the ceiling under fluorescent lights. It's coarse and fibrous, strands twisted tight, some fraying into sharp little slivers. I never make it past the first knot.

We all blend together in green, until the showers. Some are big on top, some flat as a prairie. We look, but we don't look. We glance away if someone meets our eyes. Towels gripped across our fronts as bottoms jiggle behind. We tippy-toe-skitter to the gang shower, unless it's our period. Those girls can get dressed. Sometimes we fake ours. The gym teacher makes us shower anyway. Does she keep track?

Towels gone, the flat-chested hug their elbows, showered in a spotlight of water. The girls in the clique have it all — perky breasts, curves, confidence. The rest of us side-glance; so many different chests. And nipples! We turn around once in the stream of water, then rush back to lockers. Panties over damp skin, crotch tugged free from the crack. Hook, twist, lift — breasts covered in self-conscious haste. Blouse buttoned; cardigan next. Nylons gathered up one at a time, clipped into a girdle-like garter belt, impossibly damp and sticky. Half-slip and skirt. Nearly late for the next class, sweat pours down our necks, trickles the "V" between our breasts. Our cheeks are red, but not from exercise.

white apple blossoms
scatter in the rain
fruit swells plump and red

Endless Summer

Becky and I sunbathe in baby oil, press adhesive tape "Ws" to our thighs that tan everywhere but there. The white W is for our heart throb: William. It's our summer of thirteen; rock 'n roll on the radio: *Sealed with a Kiss, Johnny Angel,* and *She Loves You, yeah, yeah, yeah.*

We camp out in the backyard in my brother's green pup tent pitched under the maple. Popcorn, pillows, and flashlights litter the tent. My transistor blares *Big Girls Don't Cry.*

frenzied wings
crickets chirring the night
come find me.

Next morning, as the sun heats up the dark tent, we fling open the door flaps to remnants of last night – a scattered deck of cards, rumpled sleeping bags, popcorn seeds in the bottom of the bowl. Our cat is out hunting this morning. We hear her little bell. I coo, *Inky. Inksby. Oh, Kitty, my Sweetieeeek* … Inky chases a gray mouse into the tent. Tiny claws scratch up Becky's back, inside her pajamas.

The tent bulges like two watermelons in a *SuperValu* bread bag. Inky runs off, we scramble out of the tent into the house. Adhesive tape dangling, white beacons of "W" blaze our thighs, and not a boy in sight.

empty tent
a mouse sleeps
in a girl's shoe

I Got my First Cavity Because of The Beatles

It all started with two by four inch
slabs of chalky-pink bubble gum
tucked behind Beatle cards
folded into waxy wrappers.

We bought the gum for the trading cards.
Paul, the cute one, with dreamy eyes.
John, like a bad boy with his long hair.
George, the quiet, thoughtful one.
Drummer Ringo, engaging and goofy.
We liked Paul the best, those eyes, that pouty mouth.

Most of the cards were printed in black and white,
a few special ones came in full color.
Four cards to a pack
and more gum.

The wrappers begged,
Collect them all.
Each card numbered on the back.
Portrait cards and group shots,
The Beatles descending airplane stairs
or swimming at the beach – shirtless!

I collected ninety-nine Beatle cards
that seventh-grade year
and stale slabs of sugared gum.
As the granddaughter of a dentist
I brushed after every meal,
a model for the ad slogan: *Look Ma – No cavities!*

I made it until I was thirteen, when The Beatles
took our country by storm.
Nearly every lunch hour, we girls trekked
across the street from junior high
to the candy store on Scott Street.
Anteed up our nickels
for Beatle cards, bad bubble gum
and my first cavity.

The Beatlettes

We're only thirteen, infatuated
with the fan frenzy on
The Ed Sullivan Show.

Paul, John, George, and Ringo
shake their radical ear-length hair.
We believe that they personally
want to hold our hand
and that makes us feel happy inside.

We form *The Beatlettes,*
a girl-band of early-teen cool.
My friends are *Paulette, Johnette,*
Georgette, and I am *Ringette.*

I take my brother's band-class drumsticks
and practice on Mother's hat box.
I stencil *The Beatlettes* on white paper
with blue Magic Marker.
I trim it and tape it to the top of the drum.

Handmade cardboard guitars
complete the ensemble,
Paulette makes sure to play left-handed.

We comb our hair forward,
shake bangs over our eyes,
and lip-sync to the 45s spinning:
> *I want to Hold Your Hand,*
> *I saw her standing there,*
> *All my Loving.*

We practice on the front lawn,
cardboard drum balanced
on an Early American chair
from the dining room.

We take our show to Horace Mann Junior High
to perform for Mr. Kalkoske,
our history teacher
who says he despises The Beatles.

In disgust, he watches us shake our hair,
strum fake guitars,
thump a 4/4 beat
as The Beatles blare from behind us.

Secretly, we think
that Mr. K is putting on his own show.
For all his scowls,
we're pretty sure the attention
makes him feel happy inside too.

The Beatlettes: Janet is Paulette, Sue is Georgette, Annette is Ringette, Deanne is Johnette

Quick, Before Someone Notices

Friday night, my parents are out. I find my mother's Gillette in the medicine cabinet, sit on the tub's edge with my feet in shallow water, and twist the double-edge blade into place. Do I go with the growth, or against it, like petting a dog the wrong way?

I soap my legs and drag the razor slowly against the grain of long brown hair, feel it tug. It takes forever to catch each hair, patch the nicks with bits of toilet paper. How far should I go? Kneecap to the top of my thigh? Back of the legs, or just the front?

clumps of hair
circle the drain
thirteen, first shave

"The first half of life is learning to be an adult —
the second half is learning to be a child."
\- Pablo Picasso

The Malmer House – Ephraim 1908-1964

It was nothing fancy. The rooms
were clean and quiet, with two stories
and eighteen rooms for rent.

A veranda welcomed tourists
for food and lodging. It was clapboard,
painted white, of course,
with a view of Eagle Bluff across the harbor
and lazy sailboats gliding by.

In the early 1960s, my family stayed there.
It reminded Dad of New England,
Cape Cod-like and family-run, reasonable.
A round silver bell sat on the front desk.
A hand-printed sign instructed: *Ring for service.*

The stairs creaked up to our room.
Railings smelled of old wood.
Dust motes drifted in shafts of sunlight.
To ten-year-old me, the oldness felt new.
Frosted pink ceiling globes cast dim light
on flowered wallpaper.
The narrow hall was covered in mottled brown carpet.

Air conditioning was an open window.
White sheer curtains breathed into the screens,
sun sparkled across the bay.
A vase stuffed with sweet-scented lilacs sat on a table.
Beds were draped in white chenille bedspreads,
down the hall, a shared bath.

Shards of Memory

Summer 1962

I'm holding a rag. We have company in the backyard. My dad bends over to pick up something, his backside rising into the air. I tear the rag in half. *Rrrrrip.*

Dad freezes. Looks at me. Then, laughs so hard he can barely stand up straight.

Spring 1963

Our neighbors gave their children a baby lamb for Easter. While we petted it, the boys next door asked what we were having at our house for Easter dinner. I told them my mom was roasting lamb. They screamed.

Autumn 1966

Dad took me to the Pilgrim Lutheran Church parking lot to teach me how to drive a stick shift. We had a little red Valiant with a hump on the trunk for the spare tire. As I learned to ease off the clutch, the car lurched and jerked across the empty lot. Dad and I laughed so hard I could barely steer. He was patient with me through every stall and jolt until, finally, I could drive smoothly.

June 1989

Now with a family of my own, just before Father's Day, we moved into a new house. As we settled in to make it feel like home, my husband mentioned wanting a new, cordless (battery) screwdriver. The kids and I bought one, wrapped it up, and gave it to him for Father's Day. When he opened it, our eight-year-old asked, *What's the big deal? Aren't they all cordless?*

THE DAY WE STEPPED INTO LIVES OF OUR OWN

Surrender

Ports Des Morts,
churning channel between
mainland and island
surges with white caps.
The wind delivers a change of season.
Spray spews across the deck,
where Lake Michigan meets the Bay.
Sails, like gulls, fly against a robust sky.
My hand pulls on the tiller to hold the heel.
The hull cuts through rollers like a good decision.
We watch a gust of wind charge the channel.
Dad shouts, *Here comes The Boss!*
I put the rail in the water
eager to hover on the edge
but only when his hand is nearby.
There's a rush of water, wind, and sails
as spring surrenders to summer.

Music of Vietnam

In Madison, a student at the UW,
I sway to the music,
Peter, Paul, and Mary at The Coliseum.
Leaving on a Jet Plane
signature song for soldiers,
captivates a thousand of us,
spellbound by their three-hour concert.
We sing together, youthful ideals –
peace, love, harmony, justice.
A generous concert with encores,
and more encores. Then, they invite us
to campus for an all-night vigil.
We sit close with Peter, Paul, and Mary in their aura
captivated like cult followers.
We sing, we cry,
and wonder where all the young men have gone,
like my brother in Vietnam and his buddies.
We wait for answers – only blowing in the wind.

UW Campus Life

Greek was out.
Demonstrations were in.
Students weren't rushing
into Rush Week,
pledging was down,
fraternities and sororities dwindling.
Students pledged instead,
to march and protest.
Cheerleaders at Yell Like Hell,
pep rally at the Union for Homecoming,
could not compete with
Hell No! We Won't Go.

Bayonets on Campus

In my brother's shadow at the same Big Ten school,
I begin freshman year, first time away from home.
The National Guard marches up Bascom Hill in formation,
they parade in unison like warriors, face shields down,
rifles with bayonets propped on shoulders.

My brother sends letters from Vietnam.
He has an M-16, hand grenades, tear gas,
and describes surprise attacks on nighttime jungle sweeps.
Mortars crack over their heads in a ball of fire.
A land mine explodes beneath a tank.

Mother writes to me of the empty nest at home,
says the quiet is deafening.
She cries for her son's safety;
she cries for my safety.
My brother writes, the headline of the

Pacific Stars and Stripes reads:
Bayonets on Campus in Madison.
As a recent grad, he jests, *That sounds about normal.*
I feel the burn of tear gas, fear guns on campus,
guards standing at attention outside my classroom door.

Police wield clubs against students.
I dodge canisters of tear gas lobbed at my dorm
as protestors run inside. I shake with fear
during riots on campus. I shake with fear
even more for my brother in Vietnam.

Star Lake After Vietnam

After the painting "Our Campsite" by Olaf Schneider, Mississauga, ON

They balance their gear in the center of the Grumman – the work-
horse of canoes. She sits in the bow, he in the stern, paddles held the
way he taught her as a kid. Every stroke churns plate-sized eddies in
the water as they glide toward a place he remembers. The only sound
is the drip of water from the blades.

They head toward an island with a shore bedded in pine needles.
Aspens rustle in the breeze. Granite boulders line the edge, and the
canoe slides over an open patch of sand, bumping gently against
the bank.

back to the world
far from blistered heat
everything green

He pitches a tent under shade trees while she gathers windfall
branches for firewood. He fries corned-beef hash and eggs over an
open flame. They eat in silence, watch an eagle circle above the pines.
After a swim, they rest on sun-warmed boulders.

He does not speak of the war but remembers childhood – winters
skiing Rib Mountain, summers fishing Lake Wausau. She recalls
family cookouts in the backyard and fireflies in the honeysuckle
hedge in July.

He fishes a little. She sunbathes. Brother and sister, a weekend away
in that time before marriage, before children, cousins, and commo-
tion, when they didn't know what was coming next.

tremolo of loons
echoes across
the dark lake

Everyday Warrior

The 1980s began with the cry of our first child, and two years later, another. This decade was a blur of burp cloths, breastfeeding, butt wiping, and never-empty laundry baskets.

I filled the freezer with bottles of breast milk; hand-pumped during my lunch break in a pink-tiled bathroom stall at work. There were no lactation rooms, no electric pumps; just me, squeezing a plastic horn with a blue rubber bulb, watching blue-tinged milk trickle into a bottle. At home, breastfeeding was a blessed pause, my only moment to catch my breath.

We were always rushing from home to the sitter or daycare, to work, and back again. And dinner? Always a question with no answer.

I was a bag lady, diaper bag slung over one shoulder, back aching as I strapped kids into car seats or carried a toddler on my hip. I wiped noses, bottoms, and tears; panicked at every fever, cough, and rash. Vacation days were used for sick-child days. I was a manager at a hospital with no time to manage myself.

Big hair. Big diaper bag. Big anxiety.

Evenings were *Hill Street Blues* while nursing; mornings, *Sesame Street* with sticky fingers and soggy Cheerios. *Bozo's Circus* played next door at our Nanny's house. Some days I felt like Bozo himself, face painted with fatigue, juggling the circus of life.

The washer whirred at 10:30 p.m., then the dryer, folding, and tip-toeing into dark bedrooms to slide clean clothes into drawers; a silent victory before midnight. Nights were short, my mind too wired to sleep until one a.m., only to be jolted awake at six to do it all again.

We were the first generation (pioneers, really) pushed by advertising and swept up in a generational transformation to become the twenty-four-hour woman:

Bring home the bacon, fry it up in a pan …

This was the decade of Super Mom and working mother guilt: I filled dozens of albums with kid photos to prove we could do it all. Luckily there were two of us. Husband and wife, we were a team.

I ended each day journaling details of their little lives: First outing, first food, first words, first steps, first toy, first day of school, and the funny things they said: When the youngest lost his first tooth, he asked where the Tooth Fairy lived. The oldest said, *Everyone knows, the Tooth Fairy is God's wife.*

Summer Boy
for Drew

Wired with energy,
you sprint across backyard,
chase red ants into their sandy holes,
pluck fistfuls of *Johnny-jump-ups*
dig in the dirt, splash in puddles,
hit a ball and run bases
around our four maple trees,
laughing with delight.

In the shadow of a tired sun,
your tanned frame drops into bed
on clean sheets,
dried smooth with summer.
Your body perspires,
breathing deep,
legs twitch,
like a firefly, you glow,
left-over light.

Bowl of Summer

Sixteen degrees below zero,
wind chill at minus thirty.
A bowl of summer
sits on the bedroom dresser.

Dried bachelor buttons
in shades of blue
and pink as bright
as their day in July,

white starbursts
of Queen Anne's Lace
press against the glass globe
from the inside out.

Sweet purple clover,
tufted globes
fluff in the middle.
July drifts across the room,

my little boy of four
holds wild bouquets
in tight fists behind his back,
Pick a hand, Mom.

Theory of Choir
(Why Choir is Essential)

Breath lifts us.
We go deep
to push notes upward.
The diaphragm
does its proper job,
restoring breath and balance
after we limp in for rehearsal,
beaten down by
the shallow breathing of rushing
from one thing to the next.

We focus on music, this night,
the ebb and flow of dynamics, text,
breathing, and more breathing,
where nothing else could possibly
clutter our heads except
the lissom line of black notes
running up and down the page,
and words catching us off our guard
as we press the two together
turning both into music.

Singing transposes us from
demanding bosses,
final exams,
ridiculous deadlines,
that nagging pain in the small curve of the back.

We are made whole again in music.
We seek the rhythm of our hearts,
find harmony in
the sum of our parts.
We chant our stories,
one note, upon another and another,
we blend as one, a collective "everyone"
sitting side by side, row upon row.

Like bricks on a path,
carefully laid down
one next to the other,
one journey of sound,
one interlocking message,
as we crescendo upward,
assembled at the seam of Here
and the Hereafter,
our scores held firmly to our chests.

Andromeda
for Anna

From her computer in Wisconsin, she peers
through a remote telescope in Australia,
travels the universe beyond the Milky Way.
She probes closer and closer to
the edge of time, the birth of light.
She drifts like the Hubble past stars
named and yet-to-be-named,
light-years from home.
Like Henrietta Leavitt who mapped
pulsing orbs in a distant sky,
my daughter glides through galaxies,
with telescope and camera to capture
what is beyond the dust of thought and idea,
to the stuff of creation.
Astronomer and photographer
she searches science in silence,
bright as the light that touches her.

Andromeda, astrophotography by Anna Kari Grunseth

Lessons and Legacies

Going to the Polls with Mother

The gray-tiled floor smells of sweeping compound. There is a wooden stage to the left, basketball hoops on either end of the room. Mother is handed a paper ballot after giving her name and address to the poll worker. We walk across the gym to a wood-framed booth with a navy-blue curtain. She pulls the drape aside, steps up to the shelf, picks up the yellow pencil tied to a long string, closes the curtain behind her. *Voting is by secret ballot,* she says. I am not allowed to look, even though I'm too young to read.

ducklings
follow the mallard
staying close

When absentee ballots are brought to the dining room at Woodside Manor, Mother, age ninety-one, is the first one in line. Her table-mates grumble, *We're too old. We don't care anymore.* Mother bristles, explains why they need to know their candidates and vote. She marks her ballot, slides it into the box, returns to the table, snaps open her newspaper to a sample ballot.

lion paces
back and forth
along the iron fence

Heirloom Quilt

Grandmother's Flower Garden,
a pattern of the past, hand-stitched
from one decade into the next,
with scraps of fabric binding
grandmother to mother to daughter.

Seven cotton hexagons, calico-ed in a circle,
are surrounded by twelve more.
A dozen bouquets of cotton flowers
are gingham-ed and striped into the quilt.
Remnants were saved from threadbare times.

Mother reads me the quilt: lavender
and yellow was a dress for the dance;
green stripes, shirts and shorts for play;
yellow and light blue, Sunday's best for church.
She points out blue and white for house dresses,
and the red-and-blue flowers of aprons.

Life's leftovers were salvaged and stitched
into *Grandmother's Flower Garden,*
each flower, a story passed on.

Grandmother's Flower Garden quilt,
made by my grandmother Mimi
(Mildred Bergh)

In My Mother's Recipe Box

In a cloud of flour, you will find
Great-Grandmother Marie, Aunt Minnie,
Grandma Mimi, and my mother
on three-by-five cards filed
in a flip-top wooden box.
Well-thumbed tabs expel paper dust,
bent edges divide tastes of the past
into breads, cookies, desserts, meats, vegetables.

In my mother's recipe box, you will find
slanted cursive written in blue fountain pen,
ingredients, directions, and temperatures
that spill onto the backs of the cards.
Aunt Minnie's powdered sugar prints
mark Sugar Cookie cutouts,
her gravy stains accent Norwegian Meatballs.

In my mother's recipe box, thumbprints smudge
Chocolate Brownies, the initials *MHB*
in the upper right corner.
I still smell them, warm from the oven,
shiny on top, moist in the middle.
Try Grandma Mimi's light Lemon Cookies,
served at tea time, and her flaky pie crust,
rolled with her one-handled rolling pin.

My mother's recipe box holds the imprint of strong women
who rolled potato dough for Lefse at Christmas.
Great-Grandma Marie's hands kneaded Julekake,
her dough stretching across four generations
and one wide ocean, escaping scarcity,
bringing recipes, seeking abundance
rising in a new land.

Rolling Pin

I lift it from the dusty box
marked "Kitchen,"
one-handled, handed down
from grandmother, to mother, to me.

It smells of Mimi's prairie pantry,
of old wood, sticky with July,
of the tall cupboards painted white
with glass knobs on the doors.

Windowed in light,
Mimi is surrounded by white flour,
white sugar, white canisters.
She wields her one-handled rolling pin,
the one for flaky pie crust
and tender lemon cookies
fed to our waiting tongues.

Smooth and wood-grained,
it smells of pie
and cookie dough.
My hands shape a round of dough,
then with the floured arm of wood,
I start at the middle and push outward —
north, south, east, west.
I guide the blunt end
lopped off a century ago
to fit in the drawer
of her prairie pantry.

At the Back Steps

During the Great Depression
they rode the rails,
knew where to find a meal.
They'd jump from freight cars
into this little prairie town.
They'd look for the white house
with the big porch. At the back steps
she invited them in, two or three at a time.
They ate meatballs rolled with nutmeg,
ginger, allspice and clove, swaddled in gravy,
with mashed potatoes and green beans,
snapped fresh from the garden, and pie.
Yes, pie! Resting on crust so flaky
it melted comfort on their tongues.
She fed them in late afternoon,
men with sad eyes — hobos,
probably with children of their own
somewhere across all those fields of dust.
Great Grandma filled empty bellies,
asked one favor: that each do a chore
in return before they hopped
the clacking wheels again,
riding the wail of the whistle
into the distance.

Marie Ruud Bergh
Madison, Minnesota, 1930s

SANDWICHED BETWEEN

Cicadas Can Reach 100 Decibels

In August crickets and grasshoppers
warn the end is near
rubbing legs and wings together.
Whirring rasp, insistent chirps
remind us how far we've traveled
in this season of sun, deep red tomatoes,
and tasseled corn.
Then, cicadas punctuate the afternoon,
a piercing buzz of late summer.

And so it was the year
my mother was hanging on
in her last season, too weak to talk.
I asked if she wanted to go
outside in her hospital bed,
she nodded yes.
I wheeled her into the hospice garden.
Together, we listened —
crickets click-clicking, grasshoppers whirring,
cicadas with their arrow of sound
voicing what's ahead
reminding us of the journey.

Marigold

Sunday school in April, we pushed needle-thin seeds into a few spoonfuls of soil pressed into paper Dixie cups.

Our third-grade hands dribbled water into the soil. When the slim seed tried to float, our thumbs poked it back into the solo garden.

In class, we talked about eggs and lambs and resurrection.

Our seeds sprouted green arrows up from the dark. Over the weeks, two shoots of green lace unfurled on a newborn stem.

By the second Sunday of May, the petite stalk stood tall in the paper cup, a spitball of a bud at the top. After Sunday school, hands cupped, we paraded into Yawkey Hall as parents gathered for coffee hour. We kids offered our mothers a simple gift for Mothers Day, a humble marigold.

This small sun of memory has kindled for seven decades. Now I pinch dry blooms, save seeds from season to season, scatter them wildly in my gardens: Mexican yellow, velvet orange, and deep-orange edged in maroon.

I trace the path of sunlight across our backyard as it rounds the garage and outlines the vegetable garden. I add splashes of yellow in hanging planters and clay pots along the front porch.

Their sharp scent drifts across the gardens, a thousand yellow suns, enough for Mother to find her way home.

The Pedicure

I sling a hand towel over my shoulder,
carry a plastic tub filled
with warm water to Dad's chair.
Let's soak your feet, soften up those nails.

I lift his size 14-narrow to my knee.
He tells me about summers
on his granddad's farm in Utica,
couldn't afford shoes, went barefoot for chores.

He tells me how his arches fell
walking miles in moccasins as a golf caddy
to earn money for Dartmouth during the Depression.
Smart enough to get in but had to work his way through.

His toenails, dense as tree bark,
are too thick to fit the clippers.
I file gently.
Then, squeezing lotion into my hands

I cradle his hardened heel in my palm,
work my thumbs up his flattened arch.
He tells me flat feet and a trick knee kept him
out of combat. He qualified for Intelligence.

He tells me he advised generals, gave daily briefings
about battles in the Pacific and Europe.
After kneading my way up his leathered sole,
I rub circles into the ball of his ninety-year-old foot.

He says it's his first pedicure,
sighs at how good it feels.
Holding his history in my hands,
I don't know it's the last time.

Cleaning Out My Parents' House

In the den, eight olive-green metal file cabinets stand at attention, four drawers high, swallowing the west light from the window. Each drawer scrapes open, packed tight with brittle manila folders.

As a teenager, I read and talked on the phone here. When my brother and I were small, Dad called us with a chickadee's high-low song. We always came running.

I pull files: warranties and instructions for every appliance bought over fifty-five years. The chest freezer from the year my appendix burst. The Sunbeam hair dryer with its plastic hood and coiled hose; Mom and I shared it, my giant rollers barely fitting beneath the shower-cap crown.

A receipt for a yellow bed tray, pink flowers painted around the edges. I brought her toast when she was sick; she brought me a tumbler of 7-Up and orange juice over ice when I had a fever. Dad's fishing pole and reel warranties, labeled and filed. Church council notes, and Mom's handwritten pages from history lectures and League of Women Voters debates. Her notes on liberal religion, philosophy, and *Gift from the Sea*, tucked into folders, edges yellowed with age. Each one a piece of their years in that house.

Manuals for the Oster blender, the electric hand beater, the black Singer sewing machine. The Cuisinart she feared; too sharp, too fast, still like new when I inherited it.

Receipts for a copper-colored stove, a GE refrigerator, the brown loopy couch where I rode the arm pretending I was Dale Evans on *The Roy Rogers Show.*

A folder labeled *Genealogy*. Our family traced back to Norway, ancestors cataloged with dates and family stories. Thick envelopes of weekly letters from my grandparents, written in longhand when long-distance calls were only for emergencies.

I open the patio door and breathe. I recycle manuals and receipts. I keep the letters. I keep the family tree.

In the back of the last drawer, I find it, a letter from Dad, never mailed. His handwriting slants downhill as his eyes fail. Complaints about Mom, worries, frustration, addressed to me, sealed in silence.

I close the drawer. Eight olive-green soldiers, ready for auction.

warm breeze
through the open door
a single chickadee calls

When a Sleepless Child

My dad drew on my face.
His big-daddy fingers
touched my forehead,
then brushed the tops of my eyelids,
down to my cheeks,
over and over.

Forehead, eyelids, cheeks.
A feather's tickle-touch.
My breath slows,
the room drifts away,
like a bird in the wind,
circles, then lifts into a dream.

Now on sleepless nights,
I envision thought-clouds
scattered across a blue sky.
Some are white, pillowed,
others dark thunderheads,
clogged with dirt of the day.

Thinking too much, they fill
the heavens in a wide-eyed chase
to nowhere.
Elusive sleep
slips into the distance,
in need of those big-daddy fingers.

Worries rise and fall,
restless in the chest,
paths I do not want to follow.
I remember his gentle, steady touch,
the lingering sweep of his fingers
across my eyelids.

The soft, slow circles
that eased me into calm.
I long for his fingers again,
for the quiet rhythm
that carries me back to dreams
and feather-light sleep.

"You live only as long as the last person who remembers you."
– Oscar Hammerstein from *Carousel*

RIVERS AND REFLECTIONS

How to Live Like a Water Lily

Wake up slowly, float in a dreamy world,
silky arms folded over your face until mid-morning,
then open wide, sun-warmed awake.
Breathe from more than one place, soft and supple.
Do not worry about today or tomorrow,
or care what others think of you.
Your radiant center is tough, strong,
nourished by water and light.
Wind and wave may engulf you,
but you can easily separate from submersion,
opening your face to the heavens.
Push back beads of wet darkness.
Move freely. Make white-water circles until afternoon,
when you fold softly back into yourself,
drowsing in the dimming daylight.

Reading a River

When canoeing,
look for ripples on the river,
focus where the water makes a "V."
When the apex points toward you,
paddle hard left or right of the point,
for that is a hidden rock that could capsize you.
See an upside-down "V" in the river?
The wide end marks rocks on either side.
Head straight down the middle between the rocks,
glide over the long tongue of water sticking out.
As roiling rapids rush by, chase the stream
through the chute, paddle with authority
through the watery mouth.
Conversations can run like whitewater,
a gush of words headed for hard knocks.
Navigate your dialogue, stay the course
even if your opponent
is the boulder that won't budge.
When differences of opinion
threaten to sink you,
don't water down your point,
steady your canoe, dig in,
paddle hard your truth.

At Moon Lake We Learn How to Listen Again

Morning is quiet.
Sun emerges thin through
a humid haze. Fog rises.
A distant rumble of thunder
growls its unrest.
Not sure if the uneasiness
is on the outside
or the inside.
Maybe it's just a truck
rolling up the back drive,
or thoughts struggling
to the surface.
Pay attention
to the rumble.
Listen.
Can you hear the water lilies open?
Did you see the loon
snag forgotten dreams
from the dark water?

Meditation in Time

On the morning-glazed lake,
I step into my kayak,
slip into the worn seat,
feet braced, knees soft.
The paddle arcs through unbroken water.
My torso swings with the cadence
of each pull and push.
I want to know the music of this water,
to forget the dissonance of this world
if only for a little while.

I paddle legato through loosestrife and arrowroot.
Wild iris wave their violet batons.
Water droplets from my paddle
are a prelude to silence.
White lilies reach in tune with the sun.
Yellow cow lilies sway among heart-shaped pads.

In a lone pine crowned with a nest,
an osprey feeds her chick ribbons of torn fish.
Her mate lands with grace,
his wings fold to join their duet.
I paddle forward in rhythm,
while time rolls back in my kayak.

Loons echo across the lake,
their voices older than time.
Their haunting calls draw me in.
I secretly watch their offspring.
The female lifts a wing to push
one baby up on her back.
For now, they are safe.
I wish it were so
for everyone, everywhere.

A Couple of Kayakers

You're fishing a cove, hidden from view,
While I paddle past islands grown over with weeds.
Purple flag irises rim the slough.
An otter swims close then under some reeds.

It's time for our picnic. I spot a new island.
I head toward a beach of blonde sand.
I radio my love of this vacant find.
You follow, our kayaks couple on land.

We forgot our swimsuits at home today,
so strip our clothes for a quick skinny dip,
frog-kick and splash, you join me to play,
entwine underwater, we drift and we slip.

Arms hug each other, my legs wrap your waist,
speed boats flash past; we wave from the water,
two bobbling heads, we tread interlaced,
giddy with giggles, we swim like the otters.

Feeling frisky at seventy, old honeymooners,
we discover we aren't too old for a nooner.

Forget-Me-Not

The Forget-Me-Not
might be forgotten
if there were just one,

so small, so blue
with a miniature yellow eye
that peers into a big world.

Thousands together
are ethereal,
a blue cloud

that settles like a tablecloth
on the forest floor
as far as you can see.

Feast on this tapestry of powder blue,
breathe in the honeyed scent
from the afternoon yawn of the sun.

Do not hurry
amid the purr of bees,
behold nothing but elfin blue

from here to the horizon,
so that you do not forget.

Ekphrastic Blue

From three paintings at the Margaret Lockwood Gallery,
Sturgeon Bay, WI

I need blue
ripples of blue, a sea of blue
rolling blue waves.

I want to float on cerulean,
tread in a pool of plain
middle-of-the-road blue.

I crave turquoise
with a hint of grass and sun,
and tranquil sky blue.

I want to fade into a curtain
of indigo, or cobalt,
the dusk of quiet space,

then wake to the palest of blue
in a gauzy sky
on a humid morning.

I need blue to wash away
the red angst of madmen,
the orange fire of bullets.

I need blue to wash away
the daily barrage of,
well, everything.

Give me every blue you have —
balm of blue,
blue   bluer   bluest.

How I See Myself

The person inside me
is a well of ability,

one leg over the monkey bars,
a blur of circles.

The person inside me
still flips cartwheels across the lawn.

The person inside me
skis double diamonds, if only in my dreams.

The person inside me
once portaged a canoe, carried a pack.

The person inside me,
though tired now, is eager

to walk a forest trail,
watch sunsets, kayak mirrored lakes

to my last breath,
to the last beat of my heart.

What We Know

At the solstice of shortening years
we enter the days rumored to be golden.
Oh, some are, those days we paddle
to the edge of summer light
across a mirror of lake under a traveling sun.

With how bright we still feel,
how can our time be more than half over
as we count children raised, meals cooked,
journeys to the woods, campfires made, trails hiked?
How will it be, going into that good night?

Those close calls — cancer, chemo, recovery
have taught us to linger longer,
hug in the kitchen,
give love pats on the bum,
drink slow sips of wine,
and know every sunset as a gift.

cherry red sunset
drips over the horizon
dessert of the day

Mozart Visits Rib Mountain

We ride the chairlift together,
I never skied with Mozart before.
Domine eis requiem, he says
Ah, the requiem! I whisper.

We scan ski runs from the top,
Allegro, don't you think? he says.
I sing a line from the fugue
head down *Birch Run,*
a black-diamond trail. Definitely, allegro.

In 4/4 rhythm I carve even turns
to the bottom of the hill,
a line of music dances from head to toes,
Mozart drives every turn.

We ski again in 4/4 time
as I spray powder into the woods,
he at the end of his run of sixteenth notes
and I finish with perfect parallel turns.

We ride up the chair again, music circling us.
Next, we choose Dusky, a blue-square intermediate,
perfect for the second movement,
Adagio, he calls.

Wide, graceful turns carve through my hips.
He and I ski until my thighs burn
with a rush of music and wind,
winter sun sinking orange to the west.
Mozart cries out, *Domine eis requiem.*

ΕPILOGUE

Today, Just Today

Memory rushes onward
like a river to a distant sea
churning in my mind
all the places I've been
and where I still want to go.

Oh, to stop. Here, now,
to dangle my feet
from the mossy bank of today,
red maples arched over me,
a crisp blue sky.

Let this cold water
rush over my tired feet.
Let me breathe
breathe in
the season of now.

I want to tame
the eddy of time,
slow the swirl of it all
the passing away
of days,
and people.

Hold the future distant
as a purpled mountain,
a horizon far away.
I am not yet ready.

Let me linger longer,
one more day,
one more week,
one more year.

NOTES ON POEMS

Banana Split Moon was inspired by a two-year-old friend who looked up at the night sky and declared the new moon a "banana moon." I couldn't resist turning it into a dessert.

Playing Paperboy is a villanelle, a French verse form made up of five tercets followed by a concluding quatrain. The first and third lines of the opening stanza alternate as refrains throughout the poem, then come together as the final couplet. (Definition adapted from the Poetry Foundation.)

Ruptured reflects a significant childhood experience as I remember it at age five. At the time, medical information was not shared with young children and the child-patient was not included in explanations or decisions. This piece is written from a child's perspective. Today, healthcare is different and information and consent are part of the process, even for children.

Haibun is used for several poems in this collection. It is an ancient Japanese form that combines brief, image-rich prose with a haiku that adds reflection or connection. See if you can find them in the book. The next note gives you a head start.

The Paint Was Still Wet is a haibun that hints at another childhood memory in the haiku. When I was four, I discovered round brown "balls" in the snow and lined them up to play until my brother, five years older, told me they were rabbit droppings. Ewww! Luckily, I was wearing mittens.

The Malmer House – Ephraim, WI, 1908-1964
Christina Malmer owned the Rest Haven Resort from 1908 to1912. It became the Malmer House under the management of her two daughters for the next 20 years as a rooming house. William Malmer

purchased it in the 1940s and operated it until 1964. (Door County Advocate archives, 1963-64.)

Meditation in Time

Midsummer's Music has brought live classical music to Door County for over three decades and partners with Write On, Door County. I was invited to write a poem inspired by a piece of music whose composer and history I did not know, letting the sounds guide the words. I read the poem at the beginning of the performance in August 2025. It also received an Honorable Mention in the Wisconsin Fellowship of Poets Dyad contest in 2025.

Ekphrastic Blue was written at the Margaret Lockwood Gallery in Sturgeon Bay, Wisconsin, as part of Write On, Door County's *Art Speaks* program, where poets visit regional galleries to let artwork inspire their writing. The poem was inspired by three of Lockwood's blue pieces, focusing on color and form. It was later published alongside her artwork in *Moss Piglet* and won second place in the Wisconsin Fellowship of Poets Triad contest.

ACKNOWLEDGEMENTS

Although poets write alone, we are sustained by community. I am grateful to the people and organizations whose friendship, collegiality, and generosity brought this collection of poems and short prose to life.

I am especially grateful to the Wisconsin Fellowship of Poets for its welcoming community, contests, and workshops; and to Write On, Door County, Jerod Santek, and the committee for the writing residencies that offered quiet, focused time to finish and refine this work. I am also thankful for Write On's *Art Speaks* program, where poets gather in Door County galleries to write ekphrastic poems under the leadership of Peter Sherrill and Carrie Sherrill, Poets Laureate of Door County, and for its workshops, which provided additional opportunities to write and grow. Deep appreciation to Peter, Carrie, and to Tori Grant Wellhouse, Vice President of the Wisconsin Fellowship of Poets, whose friendship, wise counsel, and thoughtful critique sustained me throughout the process.

I also wish to thank the Belles Lettres monthly writing group; Robin Chapman's spring workshops at Björklunden, and the weekly online community, The Raft, with Phyllis Cole-Dai for ongoing inspiration and support. Special thanks to Penny Harter, for her workshop and generous guidance on some of the Haibun included in this collection.

Thanks as well to Tom and Ethel Mortenson Davis, Estella Lauter, and Suzi Shapiro, whose encouragement, including serving as beta readers, helped shape this work. My gratitude also goes to the best elementary school anywhere, John Marshall School in Wausau, Wisconsin, where so many friendships and memories were made.

Heartfelt thanks to Judy Kneiszel for careful copyediting. Gratitude to Ruth Crocker at Elm Grove Press, who brought together my work for publication a second time, and to John Bloner, editor at *Moss Piglet*, whose monthly themed submissions stirred memories that became poems. Finally, to my husband of more than fifty years, John, and to my children Anna and Andrew and their spouses, EJ and Elisa, thank you for your love, encouragement, and for reading early drafts of poems, shaping this work in countless ways.

Photographs by: Al Langlois, Anna Kari Grunseth, Annette Langlois Grunseth

I am also grateful to the editors and curators of the journals and anthologies in which earlier versions of some of these poems appeared.

8142 Review / Hal Gruetzmacher Poetry Prize (2022): *Cicadas Can Reach 100 Decibels*

American Choral Directors Association Journal: *Theory of Choir*

Appleton Poetry Walk: *Andromeda*

Ariel Anthology (2019): *When I Was Six*

Bramble: *Andromeda, Darkroom, Junior High Gym Class*

Combat and Campus: Writing Through War: *Bayonets on Campus, Music of Vietnam, Olly, Olly Oxen Free, UW Campus Life*

Door County in Poetry: *Surrender*

Fox Cry Review: *Fooling the Tooth Fairy*

From Everywhere a Little: A Migration Anthology: *In My Mother's Recipe Box*

Halfway to the North Pole: (a Door County Anthology): *The Malmer House – Ephraim 1908-1964*

Moss Piglet: *A Couple of Kayakers, A Scar for Life, The Beatlettes, Carrot Capers, Cleaning Out My Parents' House, Crayola Cravings, Dad's Vise, Don't Lose It, Ekphrastic Blue, Every Day Warrior, Fooling the Tooth Fairy, Forget-Me-Not, Foundations, Heirloom Quilt, I Am, I Got My First Cavity Because of the Beatles, I Stand Corrected, Just for Today, Marigold, Olly, Olly Oxen Free, South Dakota – 1961, Sunday Funnies, The Father of Modification, The World at Our Fingertips, Transported*

Peninsula Pulse: *Heirloom Quilt*

Poetry of Cold: *Mozart Visits Rib Mountain*

Poetry of Presence II: *How to Live Like a Water Lily, The Pedicure*

Portage Magazine, Carroll University: *Reading a River, Where Maples Grew*

Silver Birch Press: *Cicadas Can Reach 100 Decibels*

Soundings: Door County in Poetry: *Surrender*

The Poeming Pigeon/The Poetry Box: *Theory of Choir*

Wisconsin Fellowship of Poets/Calendar: *At Moon Lake We Learn How to Listen Again, At the Back Steps, Banana Split Moon, Cherry Red Sunset Haiku, Ekphrastic Blue (Triad contest, 2nd place)*

ABOUT THE AUTHOR

 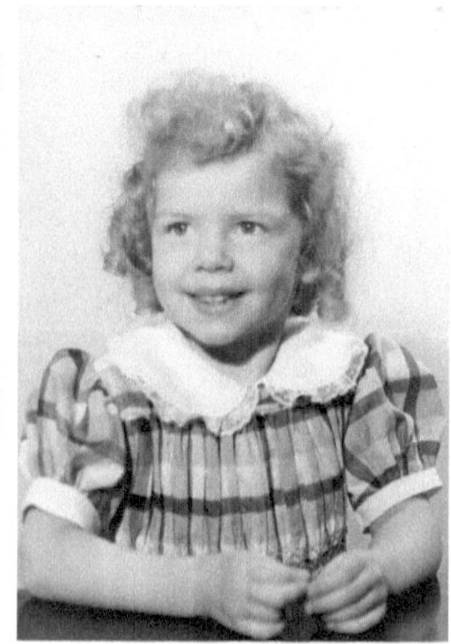

Annette Langlois Grunseth is a Wisconsin poet and memoirist whose work explores Midwestern childhood, memory, and place. She received a Pushcart Prize nomination for *Becoming Trans-Parent: One Family's Journey of Gender Transition* and a Gold Medal from the Military Writers Society of America for *Combat and Campus: Writing Through War*. A winner of the Hal Gruetzmacher Poetry Prize, she is recognized by the Wisconsin Fellowship of Poets and the Wisconsin Academy of Sciences, Arts & Letters. Her poems appear in *Poetry of Presence II*, *Love Is For All of Us*, *Silver Birch Press*, and other literary anthologies.

Her writing turns ordinary places such as five-and-dime stores, sidewalks, backyards, and schoolyards into poems and short prose that explore family, belonging, and how memory gathers meaning over time. *Summer Days at the Five and Dime* follows this journey from childhood into adulthood in a close-knit Midwestern town.

She lives in Northeast Wisconsin, where she finds inspiration while biking trails or paddling her kayak.

www.annettegrunseth.com